100 QUESTIONS about EXTREME WEATHER

and all the answers too!

Written and Illustrated by
Simon Abbott

PETER PAUPER PRESS, INC.
White Plains, New York

PETER PAUPER PRESS

In 1928, at the age of twenty-two, Peter Beilenson began printing books on a small press in the basement of his parents' home in Larchmont, New York. Peter—and later, his wife, Edna—sought to create fine books that sold at "prices even a pauper could afford."

Today, still family owned and operated, Peter Pauper Press continues to honor our founders' legacy of quality, value, and fun for big kids and small kids alike.

Designed by Heather Zschock

Published by Peter Pauper Press, Inc.
202 Mamaroneck Avenue
White Plains, New York 10601 USA

Published in the United Kingdom and Europe by Peter Pauper Press, Inc.
c/o White Pebble International
Unit 2, Plot 11 Terminus Rd.
Chichester, West Sussex PO19 8TX, UK

Library of Congress Cataloging-in-Publication Data

Names: Abbott, Simon, 1967- author, illustrator.
Title: 100 questions about extreme weather / written and illustrated by Simon Abbott.
Other titles: One hundred questions about extreme weather
Description: White Plains, New York : Peter Pauper Press, Inc., [2020] | Series: 100 questions about... | Audience: Ages 7+ | Audience: Grades 2-3 | Summary: "This illustrated children's book describes extreme weather phenomena--including hurricanes, tornadoes, heat waves, and blizzards--through a series of questions and answers"-- Provided by publisher.
Identifiers: LCCN 2019031631 | ISBN 9781441331281 (hardcover)
Subjects: LCSH: Severe storms--Miscellanea--Juvenile literature. | Weather--Miscellanea--Juvenile literature. | Natural disasters--Miscellanea--Juvenile literature.
Classification: LCC QC941.3 .A28 2020 | DDC 551.55--dc23
LC record available at https://lccn.loc.gov/2019031631

ISBN 978-1-4413-3128-1
Manufactured for Peter Pauper Press, Inc.
Printed in Hong Kong

7 6 5 4 3 2 1

Visit us at www.peterpauper.com

THE WEATHER AFFECTS US ALL.

On a good day, we can enjoy the sunshine at the beach, or ski over snow on a mountaintop.

On a bad day, hurricanes and tornadoes can cause devastation, and floods can wipe out crops and wash away homes. Lightning storms, blizzards, sandstorms, heat waves, and other forms of extreme weather can wreak havoc.

Let's take a look at the deadliest lightning, the fiercest winds, and the most torrential downpours.

Are you ready to face the elements?

WEATHER AROUND THE WORLD

Let's start at the beginning, to learn about the planet's extraordinary climate.

First things first. What is weather?
Weather is the daily condition of the air, or **atmosphere**, anywhere around the world.

TROPOSPHERE

6 MILES
(10 KM)

EARTH

What is atmosphere?
This is the wide band of air that surrounds planet Earth. It has several different layers, but weather almost always happens in the lowest layer, a space called the cloud layer or **troposphere**.

Why is weather important?
Weather is vital to our well-being. It controls our water supply and the growth of our food crops. It affects our comfort and safety. Harsh weather is the biggest natural killer on the planet.

4

What is extreme weather?
Extreme weather is weather gone *bad*. It's weather that puts life and property at risk, and/or has a major impact on the environment, causing floods, wildfires, mudslides, or avalanches.

Is the sun the mastermind behind our weather?
Yes! It's in charge of every aspect of our weather. The sun heats the Earth's land and water. This heat is absorbed, then released to warm the atmosphere, which causes the air to move. This creates wind, which changes the weather. When the sun's heat hits the oceans, it causes water to evaporate (or turn into steam, also known as water vapor). The water vapor is held in the atmosphere. As the air cools, this water falls back to the earth as rain or snow.

FACT OR FICTION?

What's the difference between weather and climate?

Weather is what it's like outside from day to day. **Climate** is the average weather experienced over time in an area of the world. Among other things, climate is affected by how far a place is from the **equator**.

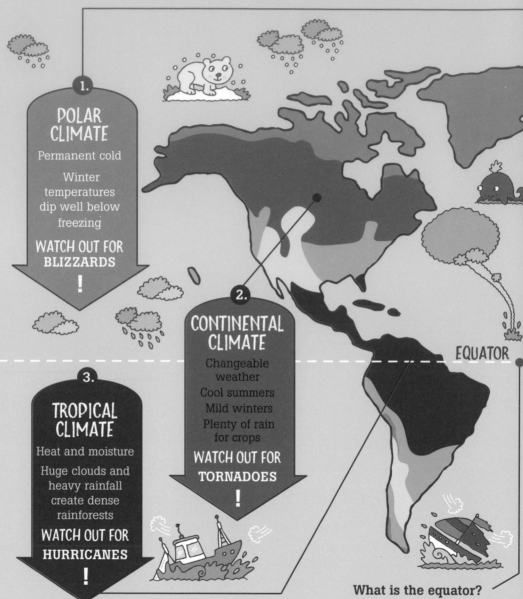

1.

POLAR CLIMATE

Permanent cold

Winter temperatures dip well below freezing

WATCH OUT FOR **BLIZZARDS**

!

2.

CONTINENTAL CLIMATE

Changeable weather
Cool summers
Mild winters
Plenty of rain for crops

WATCH OUT FOR **TORNADOES**

!

3.

TROPICAL CLIMATE

Heat and moisture

Huge clouds and heavy rainfall create dense rainforests

WATCH OUT FOR **HURRICANES**

!

EQUATOR

What is the equator?
Take a look at the map! The equator is an imaginary circle that divides the Earth into two halves called the northern and southern hemispheres.

What difference does the equator make to the world's weather?
Regions near the equator get more direct sun and are hotter. Sunlight is spread out in areas far from the equator, such as the north and south poles, which makes these places much colder.

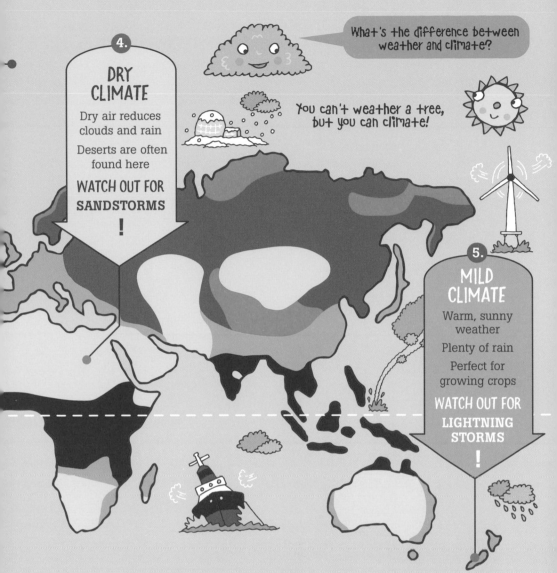

What other factors affect a region's climate and weather?

The oceans warm up and cool down much more slowly than land. Areas near the sea are therefore cooler in the summer and warmer in the winter, compared to places inland. Areas at great heights are cooler and more unpredictable too. The top of Mount Everest, the world's highest mountain, is over 29,029 feet (8,848 m) above sea level. Here, temperatures drop to a rock bottom –33°F (–36°C) in winter. Severe storms and high winds can also appear suddenly the higher up you go.

Finally, wind direction (or **prevailing wind**) influences a region's climate. If wind blows in over the sea, you'll encounter moist air and regular rainfall. Desert climates experience dry wind that has blown in over land.

WET 'N' WILD!

Grab your umbrella and pull on your rain boots! Let's splash through the statistics and get the details on rainbows and rainfall! Then, let's see what happens when rain goes rogue.

How is rain created?

Do you remember that the sun heats the oceans, then water evaporates into the air? The tiny droplets of water in the air form clouds. As clouds take on more and more water, these drops become bigger and heavier until they fall out of the sky as rain, sleet, or snow. Rain clouds hold huge amounts of water, which makes them dense and dark. The heaviest rain falls from the darkest clouds!

How is rainfall measured?

Scientists use a **rain gauge**, which is a funnel that empties water into a cylinder. (Then the scientists measure how many inches of water are in the cylinder to figure out how much rain fell.) The first known rainfall records were kept by the Ancient Greeks over 2,500 years ago!

Where is the wettest place on Earth?
That record goes to Mawsynram in India, with an amazing annual rainfall of over
467 inches (1,187 cm). That's taller than a telephone pole!

Why do they get so much rain?
Moisture sweeps in from the Bay of Bengal, and the resulting rainclouds are unable
to escape over the Himalayan mountain range to the north, so they stay and rain
on Mawsynram. Locals carry on with their daily chores by wearing waterproof
umbrella shields, called "knups."

Where is the driest place on the planet?
You'll find this in . . . wait for it . . . Antarctica! The McMurdo Dry Valleys receive
little or no rainfall. They are extremely dry, as they're protected from ice and snow
by high mountains and super-strong winds. In fact, scientists believe these valleys
are the closest thing we have on Earth to Mars!

Rain is essential for drinking water and to grow crops. When is rain not so helpful?

Acid rain forms when water vapor in the air reacts with chemicals given off by some factories and vehicles. Acid rain can poison soil, destroy forests, and even wear away stone buildings.

What other ways can rain be destructive?

Too much rain can submerge land in water or even wipe out entire cities. This is called a **flood**. Floods can damage buildings, destroy crops and animals, spread dangerous diseases, and disrupt a clean water supply.

What was the world's deadliest flood?

China's Yangtze River flooded in 1931, and this was one of the worst natural disasters in history. An estimated 3.7 million people were killed. Starvation was the biggest killer, as the region's rice fields were devastated, and the polluted water spread diseases.

What can protect communities from flooding?

People build structures that can hold floodwaters back, make them flow in a different direction, and safely contain extra water. Healthy forests and wetlands play a big part in preventing floods.

WHAT SHOULD I DO IF I'M CAUGHT IN A FLOOD?

1. Evacuate with your family to high ground.

2. Don't walk, swim, or drive through water.

3. Avoid bridges over fast flowing water.

4. If you are trapped in a building go to the highest level. Don't take shelter in a closed attic, and don't climb onto the roof if at all possible.

5. Don't use or touch any electrical equipment if it is wet.

6. Only return to your house once the authorities have said it is safe to do so.

Let's cheer ourselves up with a colorful rainbow! How is this amazing natural sight formed?

A rainbow is a stunning visual effect. White sunlight passes through falling rain. The raindrops bend the light and split it into all the colors of the spectrum. Rainbows are only seen on showery, sunny days, when gaps in the clouds let the sun shine through the rain.

WHITE SUNLIGHT

REFLECTED LIGHT IN 7 COLORS

WATER IN THE AIR

BOLT OUT OF THE BLUE

Thunder clouds are rolling in! It's time to get the essential information on electrical storms.

How do lightning bolts happen?
Lightning is a dazzling flash of electricity produced in a thunderstorm. These electrical charges are created when ice and water in the storm clouds rub together. Each bolt can contain up to one billion volts of electricity!

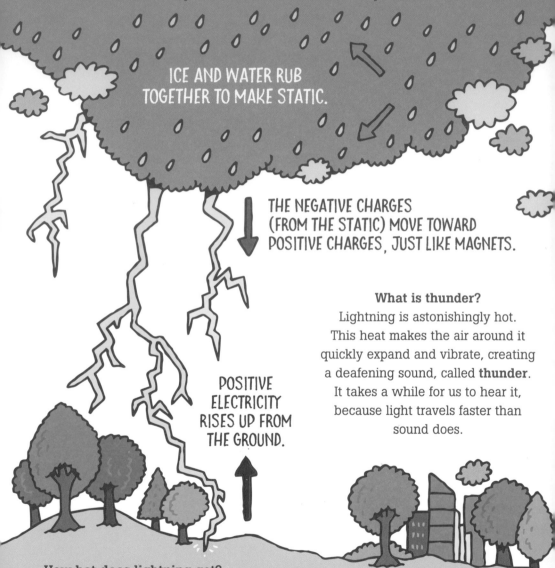

ICE AND WATER RUB TOGETHER TO MAKE STATIC.

THE NEGATIVE CHARGES (FROM THE STATIC) MOVE TOWARD POSITIVE CHARGES, JUST LIKE MAGNETS.

What is thunder?
Lightning is astonishingly hot. This heat makes the air around it quickly expand and vibrate, creating a deafening sound, called **thunder**. It takes a while for us to hear it, because light travels faster than sound does.

POSITIVE ELECTRICITY RISES UP FROM THE GROUND.

How hot does lightning get?
It can reach scorching temperatures of 53,500°F (30,000°C)! The surface of the sun is chilly in comparison, reaching just 10,340°F (5,700°C) on the thermometer!

How can I figure out how far away I am from a lightning strike?
First, make sure you're safely indoors! Then, just do the math. Count the seconds between the lightning flash and the sound of thunder. Then divide the number of seconds by 5 to work out the distance in miles. (Divide by 3 to figure it out in km!)

It always seems that lightning disappears in a flash!
How quickly does lightning move?
According to scientists, the speed of visible lightning, or the part we can see, is about 200,000,000 mph (300,000,000 kph). That's roughly half the speed of light!

HOW SHOULD I KEEP MYSELF SAFE?

In the USA alone, an average of 27 people per year die by lightning strikes. To keep yourself safe in a thunderstorm:

If you can, go indoors quickly.

Avoid electrical equipment.

Protect your pets by keeping them indoors.

Stay away from exterior windows and doors.

Avoid open fields and hilltops.

Keep clear of tall, isolated trees.

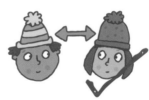

If you're in a group, stay about 15 feet (5m) from each other.

Stay away from water, wet items, and metal objects like fences and poles.

Did any lucky people ever survive a "bolt from the blue"?
Let's hear it for ex-park ranger, Roy C. Sullivan who survived not one but SEVEN lightning strikes. Throughout these extraordinary escapes, he lost his big toenail, eyebrows, and most of his hair (twice) . . . but he lived to tell the tale. He was no flash in the pan!

FACT OR FICTION?

What happens when lightning strikes water?

When lightning strikes a lake, pool, or ocean, the electricity quickly spreads outward across the surface. This means if you happen to be swimming, you stand a good chance of getting zapped, even if you're not directly struck! Being in a boat doesn't help either, as lightning could strike anything from the mast to the boat's radio, which can channel that electricity and zap those on board. So either way, don't risk it—get out of the water and stay safe!

FREAK FOG AND STARTLING SMOG

Hold your face close to this page.
We're about to go through some serious smog and fog!

What causes fog?

Fog is basically a cloud at ground level. It happens when water vapor in the air condenses (turns into water droplets) at a cool temperature. The droplets form around bits of dust, ice, or salt and create a cloud: fog! For example, here's how **advection fog** blows in from the sea:

3. the moisture in the lowest layer of air condenses and forms water droplets, or fog.

1. Warm and humid air blows in from the ocean.

2. Colder sea surface cools the air above it.

What did the fog say to the valley?

I mist you!

Are there different types of fog?
I'll say! Take a look at these options:

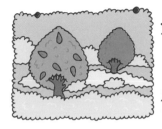

Radiation Fog
This is a very common fog usually seen around winter. It forms overnight when the air is cooler, but when the sun rises and begins to warm the air, the fog disappears.

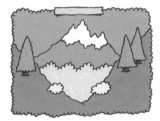

Valley Fog
Dense, cold air drifts into a valley from the surrounding mountains, then condenses and forms fog.

Advection Fog
This fog is formed when warm, moist air is cooled as it moves over a cold surface. It could happen over snowy ground, or when tropical air travels over cool water.

Upslope Fog
When wind blows up a slope, the air cools as it rises. Moisture in the air then condenses to form a fog.

Evaporation Fog
This fog is the result of cold air passing over warm water, or moist land.

Freezing Fog
When temperatures are at or below freezing, the tiny droplets in fog freeze instantly as they hit exposed surfaces such as sidewalks, roads, vehicles, and stairs. This can cause black ice (ice that's difficult to see) on roads, and can even ground aircraft.

Is fog ever useful?

It can be! In the North African country of Morocco, mesh nets on Mount Boutmezguida "catch" clouds of fog and condense it into a supply of clean drinking water for 15 villages.

During the American Revolutionary War, the Continental Army was surrounded by British troops, who expected them to surrender. Fortunately, a heavy fog descended, and the American troops were able to make a break for it. As the fog lifted, the Brits were amazed to see that the Continental Army had escaped!

BUS STOP

38 55 48

"FOG"
by Carl Sandburg

the fog comes
on little cat feet.
It sits looking
over harbor and city
on silent haunches
and then moves on.

LONDON DAILY NEWS

SMOG EXCLUSIVE!

READ ALL ABOUT IT!

Can fog be dangerous?

Yes. Dense fog causes flight cancellations, multi-car pileups on freeways, and even shipwrecks! One of history's worst maritime disasters happened in heavy fog on the St. Lawrence River in Canada.

What about smog?

On December 5, 1952, a fog smothered London, and soon began to mix with the tons of soot pumped into the air by the city's factories, chimneys, and vehicles, forming smog. The smog was so thick that Londoners could barely see their feet as they walked. The toxic fog began to lift four days later, but over 4,000 people lost their lives, with many more having trouble breathing.

What is a fog bow?

These weather wonders are also known as white rainbows, cloud bows, or ghost rainbows (spooky!). They are similar to regular rainbows, but happen when fog or clouds are full of tiny water droplets, rather than large raindrops.

NOW FOR THE WEATHER FORECAST!

We may not be able to see into the future, but we have some surefire ways of predicting our weather. Let's take a look!

Is there a name for the science of weather and climate?
Certainly! It's called **meteorology**. It comes from the Greek words *meteoros* (meaning "in the air") and *logia* (meaning to discuss, study, and explain).

What does a meteorologist do?
They are scientists who observe, explain, and forecast our weather. They use their research and data from the atmosphere to make predictions about future weather patterns and warn people about extreme weather conditions.

How do meteorologists gather all their information?

Measurements of atmospheric conditions are taken on and above the Earth's surface, 24 hours a day. Meteorologists use satellites, weather stations, aircraft, ships, radar, weather balloons, and buoys to gather worldwide data. These observations are transmitted to centers around the world and fed into huge super-computer systems. These are the starting blocks that some complicated math computers use to predict the future activity of the atmosphere.

TODAY

MON	TUES	WED	THUR	FRI	SAT	SUN
HIGH 80°F	HIGH 70°F	HIGH 60°F	HIGH 50°F	HIGH 65°F		
LOW 60°F	LOW 45°F	LOW 35°F	LOW 35°F	LOW 50°F	LOW 60°F	LOW 70°F

Why is it important to predict the weather?

Weather forecasts help keep us safe by warning us of extreme weather approaching. Forecasts can help farmers decide whether to plant, water, or protect their crops. They allow businesses to plan for transport problems, and let energy companies estimate future needs. They can also help you choose whether to have a picnic in a snowstorm, or go skiing in a heat wave!

How long have people been predicting the weather?

Over 2,300 years ago, the Greek philosopher Aristotle wrote a study called "*Meteorologica*," where he looked at weather events such as hail, hurricanes, evaporation, and earthquakes. But it wasn't until the 17th century that a more scientific path was taken. In 1643, the Italian Evangelista Torricelli discovered that air pressure affected the weather. He invented the **barometer** to measure changes in air pressure. This device is still used in weather forecasting today.

TORRICELLI

What goes up when the rain comes down?

An umbrella!

FAHRENHEIT

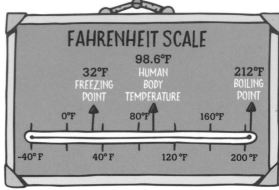

FAHRENHEIT SCALE

	98.6°F	
32°F FREEZING POINT	HUMAN BODY TEMPERATURE	212°F BOILING POINT

0°F   80°F   160°F

-40°F   40°F   120°F   200°F

Who invented the thermometer?

The physicist Daniel Fahrenheit! He came up with the mercury thermometer over 300 years ago, as well as the temperature scale that bears his name. (Celsius came later.)

What is the future of meteorology?

At present, our weather forecasts are only reliable about a week into the future. The goal is to create more detailed long-term forecasts. Scientists are working on a technique called **ensemble forecasting**. In this system, multiple forecasts are run on super-computers, each with a slightly different starting point. This will allow meteorologists to predict major weather events far into the future, and allow people to prepare for the worst.

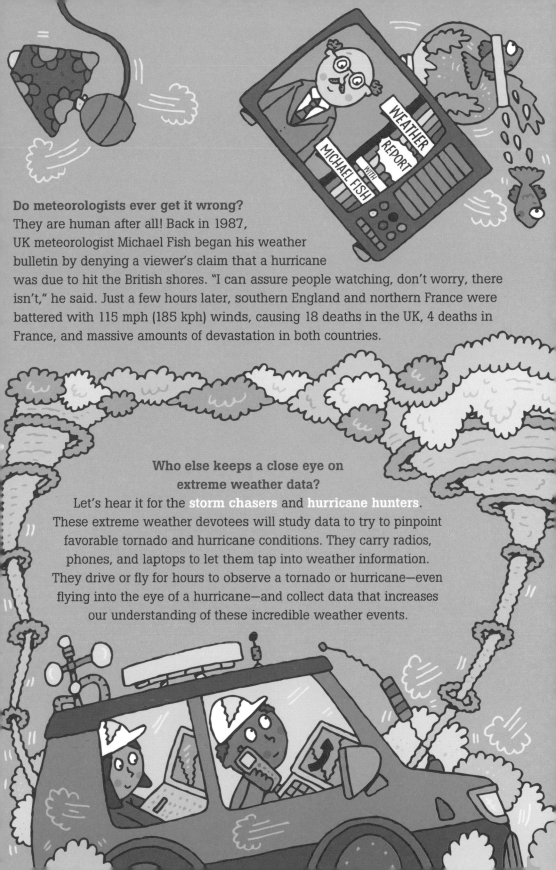

Do meteorologists ever get it wrong?
They are human after all! Back in 1987,
UK meteorologist Michael Fish began his weather
bulletin by denying a viewer's claim that a hurricane
was due to hit the British shores. "I can assure people watching, don't worry, there isn't," he said. Just a few hours later, southern England and northern France were battered with 115 mph (185 kph) winds, causing 18 deaths in the UK, 4 deaths in France, and massive amounts of devastation in both countries.

Who else keeps a close eye on extreme weather data?
Let's hear it for the storm chasers and hurricane hunters.
These extreme weather devotees will study data to try to pinpoint favorable tornado and hurricane conditions. They carry radios, phones, and laptops to let them tap into weather information. They drive or fly for hours to observe a tornado or hurricane—even flying into the eye of a hurricane—and collect data that increases our understanding of these incredible weather events.

WEATHER REPORT WITH MICHAEL FISH

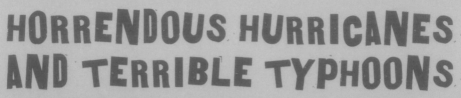

HORRENDOUS HURRICANES AND TERRIBLE TYPHOONS

Let's get up close with some terrifying tropical storms. Hold on to your hats . . . it's going to be a bumpy ride!

What's the difference between a hurricane, a typhoon, and a cyclone? Same things . . . different places! Here's all you need to know:

Hurricane   North Atlantic, Central North Pacific, Eastern North Pacific

Typhoon   Northwest Pacific

Cyclone   South Pacific, Indian Ocean

What's so bad about these storms?
They claim more lives each year than any other storm.
When a full-blown hurricane hits land, buildings are flattened,
trees ripped up, and cars get flung into the air.

Wow! How fast can the wind blow?
To be classed as a hurricane, a tropical storm has to reach 74 mph (119 kph). Top billing goes to Hurricane Patricia, which checked in at 215 mph (346 kph) over the Pacific Ocean in 2015.

Sounds devastating! Did the hurricane make it from the ocean to land?
I'm afraid so! Patricia hit Mexico as a Category 4 hurricane. It wiped out 10,000 homes, knocked down power poles, and ravaged 100,000 acres of crops. The bill for the damage totaled $325 million.

Along with the wind comes the rain.
How much water can a hurricane hold?
In 2017, Hurricane Harvey first sounded pretty tame, crawling toward the coast of Texas at just 5 mph (8 kph). However, it caused devastating floods by depositing around 60 inches (152 cm) of rain in just four days. That's over half the height of your front door!

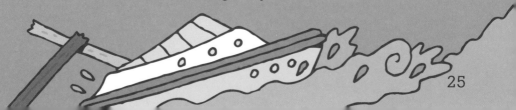

How do hurricanes happen?

They begin over warm, tropical oceans as small thunderstorms near the equator. If the water is over 80°F (27°C), warm, moist air swirls upward, cools, forms clouds, and drifts back down to start the cycle again. The winds pick up speed, the clouds grow, and a spiraling storm forms.

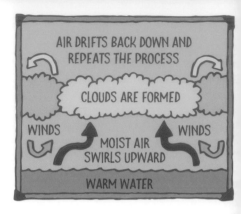

AIR DRIFTS BACK DOWN AND REPEATS THE PROCESS

CLOUDS ARE FORMED

WINDS   WINDS

MOIST AIR SWIRLS UPWARD

WARM WATER

How big can a hurricane get?

These storms are usually around 300 miles (483 km) wide. A large size doesn't always create the most powerful storm. 1992's Hurricane Andrew is considered a small storm, with rainbands that jutted out 100 miles (160 km) from its center, but it hit Florida as a Category 5 storm with 165 mph (270 kph) winds. This devastating hurricane killed 65 people and wrecked around 63,000 homes.

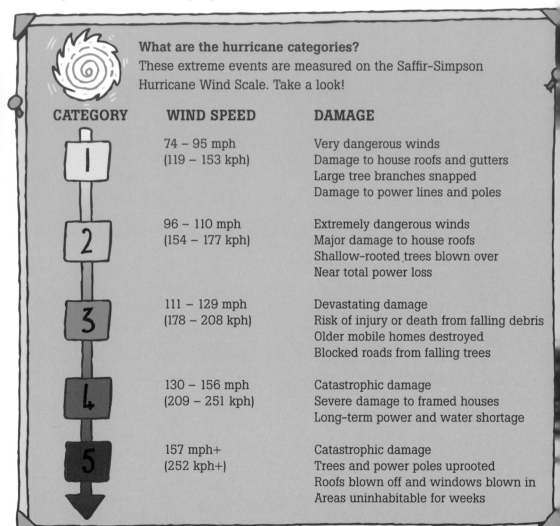

What are the hurricane categories?

These extreme events are measured on the Saffir–Simpson Hurricane Wind Scale. Take a look!

CATEGORY	WIND SPEED	DAMAGE
1	74 – 95 mph (119 – 153 kph)	Very dangerous winds Damage to house roofs and gutters Large tree branches snapped Damage to power lines and poles
2	96 – 110 mph (154 – 177 kph)	Extremely dangerous winds Major damage to house roofs Shallow-rooted trees blown over Near total power loss
3	111 – 129 mph (178 – 208 kph)	Devastating damage Risk of injury or death from falling debris Older mobile homes destroyed Blocked roads from falling trees
4	130 – 156 mph (209 – 251 kph)	Catastrophic damage Severe damage to framed houses Long-term power and water shortage
5	157 mph+ (252 kph+)	Catastrophic damage Trees and power poles uprooted Roofs blown off and windows blown in Areas uninhabitable for weeks

I've heard about the "eye" of a hurricane. What is that?

This is a circular area of calm weather at the center of a hurricane. As the eye passes over land, you'll experience clear skies and light winds. The center is surrounded by the **eyewall**. This is a ring of colossal thunderstorms where the most destructive weather occurs.

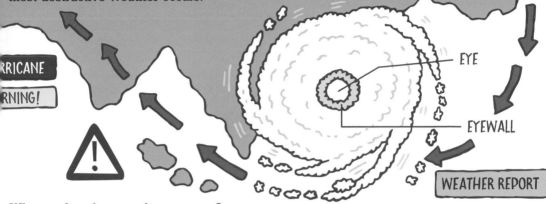

Why are hurricanes given names?

Simple! They are easier to remember and to communicate. It also stops any confusion when more than one hurricane is whirling around the world at the same time. The practice is now handled by the World Meteorological Association. Storm names are taken from an approved list in alphabetical order, with boys' and girls' titles taken in turns and repeating every six years. If a hurricane was particularly destructive, that name is crossed off the list. So, no more Hurricane Sandy, Irene, Katrina, or Rita!

WILD WEATHER FACTS

Let's dive into the record books and discover fascinating facts about our weird and wonderful weather.

Where's the windiest place on Earth?

It depends how you measure it! But some challengers to the title include Barrow Island in Australia, with the strongest single gust of 253 mph (408 kph) during a cyclone. A strong but unofficial contender would be Oklahoma, with wind during a tornado clocking in at 318 mph (512 kph). If we're talking an average wind speed, then Cape Denison in Antarctica should be in the running, with a record windy hour averaging 95 mph (153 kph).

Which sizzling spot gets the gold medal for top temperatures?

The Hottest Place on the Planet prize is awarded to Death Valley in California. In the summer of 1913, air temperatures reached a sweltering 134°F (57°C), in the appropriately named Furnace Creek. Phew!

Just to compare, what is the average temperature on planet Earth?
It's 57°F (14°C).

Where's the coldest place on Earth?

The lowest temperature ever recorded is –133.6°F (–92°C) in Antarctica. You'd get frostbite in just five minutes! The coldest inhabited place on the planet is the village of Oymyakon, in Russia. Villagers enjoy just three hours of daylight each day in the winter, and all year long they keep their cars running so the batteries don't freeze!

Where's the sunniest spot on the planet where people live?

Surprisingly, we're heading north to Ellesmere Island in Canada—almost to the North Pole! Although the temperatures are *very* low, you'd be able to enjoy over 15 hours of sunshine each day in May. In winter, however, the sun doesn't even appear over the horizon for four months!

Can our supply of sunshine be put to good use?

Sure! The Atacama Desert, in Chile, is the driest non-polar spot on Earth. In fact, in Arica, Chile, not a single raindrop fell from 1903 to 1918. It's the perfect place to test out harnessing energy from the sun. The Tierra Atacama Hotel has done just that, and powers its whole complex day and night with its 588 solar panels.

Which record-breaking neighborhood is in the running for the most snowfall in 24 hours?

Measuring snow is rather tricky! However, the official US record was set in 1921, when a blizzard dropped 6.3 feet (1.92 m) on Silver Lake, Colorado. That's as tall as a basketball player!

Let's stay with the wet world records! What's the most rainfall recorded in a day?

When Cyclone Denise passed through Foc-Foc in the Southern Indian Ocean in 1966, it dumped 71.8 inches (182 cm) of rain in just 24 hours. If it rained that much in your kitchen, your fridge would be completely underwater!

WEIRDEST WEATHER!

Which event wins the "Wacky Wet Weather" Challenge Cup?
We can hand that prize to the notorious "Red Rain" of Kerala. Back in 2001, this Indian state experienced mysterious monsoon rains. These downpours were blood red! At first, scientists blamed this phenomenon on an exploding meteor. However, further research concluded that the vibrant rain was caused by color-making spores from seaweed-like algae.

HEAVIEST HAILSTONE

FACT OR FICTION?

Are hailstones harmful?
You bet! The heaviest hailstone weighed in at a whopping 2.25 pounds (1 kg) during a violent hailstorm hitting Bangladesh in 1986. That's heavier than a basketball! No wonder the storm claimed the lives of 92 people.

ICE, ICE BABY!

Wrap up warm! We're about to chill out with some frozen facts!

How is snow made?
When the air is cold, instead of turning into rain, moisture in the clouds freezes into ice crystals. These crystals join together and take about an hour to travel to the ground as **snow**, at 1–4 mph (1.6–6.4 kph).

FACT OR FICTION?

It is *really* true that no two snowflakes are the same?
It's true! This is for a couple of reasons. First, it's in the formation. Each crystal starts out as a speck of dust or pollen. This catches airborne water vapor, which freezes into a tiny hexagonal snowflake-shape. Other frozen water molecules attach to this crystal randomly, taking on unique forms, depending on the temperature and humidity. Second, it's in the way they fall: snowflakes can strike each other and freeze together or break off bits of one another to form completely new shapes.

Where is the snowiest place in the world?

Let's hear it for Aomori, in Japan, which shivers under an average 26 feet (8 m) of snowfall every year. That's taller than a house!

CHINA

RUSSIA

N. KOREA

S. KOREA

JAPAN

We all love sledding and snowball fights! Can too much snow be a bad thing?

Absolutely! The Blizzard of 1888 hit the Northeastern US without warning and became a major disaster. New York City was buried under about 4 feet (1.2 m) of snow, and winds averaging 40 mph (130 kph) brought down power lines and created 50-foot-high (15 m) snowdrifts. New Yorkers were helpless as they became stranded on the street, in transit cars, and at work. Over 400 people lost their lives to the storm.

What is an ice storm?

Freezing rain concentrates on the ground and other surfaces to form ice.
This can add a huge weight to trees and power lines, and can bring them
crashing down. Back in 1998, a destructive ice storm hit New England and Canada.
This devastating event caused almost 40 deaths, with a damage bill running into
billions of dollars. Millions of maple and apple trees were destroyed by the ice,
blighting the productions of these crops for many years.

How are hailstones formed?

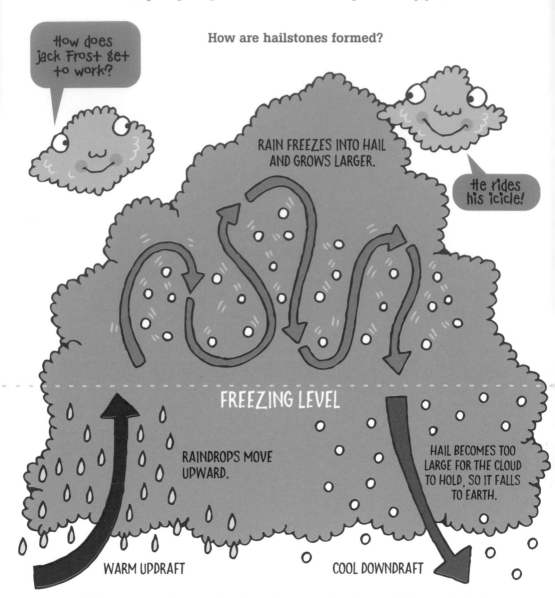

Hailstorms need storm clouds and severe, freezing, whirling wind to form.
The ice crystals inside the cloud get hurled up and down, increasing the frozen
layers on each crystal. These layers turn the tiny crystals into hailstones.

What size can hailstones reach?

Typical hailstones range from the size of a pea to the size of a marble, but they can be much larger. During a destructive thunderstorm in 2010, a record-breaking hailstone fell on Vivian, South Dakota. This frozen whopper measured an incredible 8 inches (20 cm) in diameter. That's almost as large as a grapefruit! Ouch!

How dangerous can hailstorms be?

A hailstorm that hit India in 1888 was one of the deadliest weather events in history. This fatal storm killed 246 people with hailstones as large as oranges.

TERRIBLE TWISTERS!

Let's follow a tornado's trail of destruction and get the lowdown on these wildly whirling winds.

What is a tornado?

It's a terrifying vertical funnel of rotating air, featuring super-powerful winds. These funnels are transparent but become visible as the cloud's water droplets condense, or if dust and debris is sucked up as it goes.

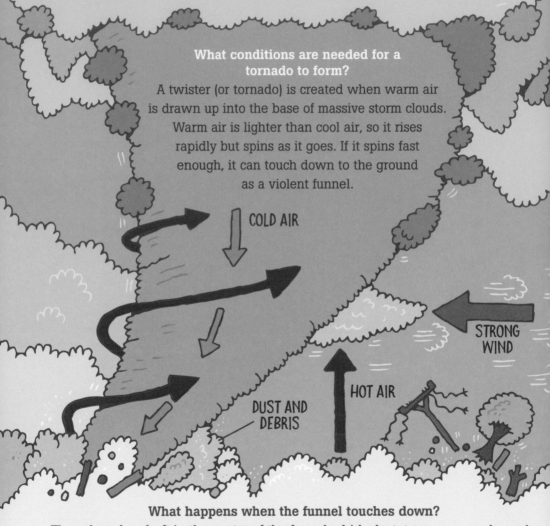

What conditions are needed for a tornado to form?

A twister (or tornado) is created when warm air is drawn up into the base of massive storm clouds. Warm air is lighter than cool air, so it rises rapidly but spins as it goes. If it spins fast enough, it can touch down to the ground as a violent funnel.

COLD AIR

STRONG WIND

HOT AIR

DUST AND DEBRIS

What happens when the funnel touches down?

The colossal updraft in the center of the funnel whirls dust, trees, cars, and people high into the air. The ferocious winds turn debris into deadly missiles, and houses in the twister's path can be reduced to matchsticks and rubble in minutes.

What is the average wind speed of a tornado?
Most tornadoes have wind speeds under 113 mph (82 kph). However,
the 2013 El Reno tornado in Oklahoma clocked up a super-speedy gust of
296 mph (476 kph). Tornadoes usually travel along the ground at 30 mph
(50 kph) and come to a halt after 6 miles (10 km). Twisters aren't that
easy to study though, as they often destroy any meteorological
instruments in their path!

How big do these twisters get?
We're heading back to the El Reno tornado. This super-sized twister
measured a record-breaking 2.6 miles (4 km) wide. That's the same as
38 NFL football fields! Eight people lost their lives, including four storm chasers
who were caught off guard. Most twisters are about 660 feet (200 m) wide.

Which places are most likely to be hit by tornadoes?

The United States tops the twister count, with an average of 1,200 tornadoes per year. Within the United States, there's a region known as **Tornado Alley**, located in the south-central plains of the country (specifically from Texas northward to Iowa and eastward to western Ohio). The other most likely place in the US to be hit by tornadoes is Florida, due to the number of daily thunderstorms in the state. Of the roughly 1,200 tornadoes in the US per year, 66 of them take place in Florida, and over 680 take place in Tornado Alley.

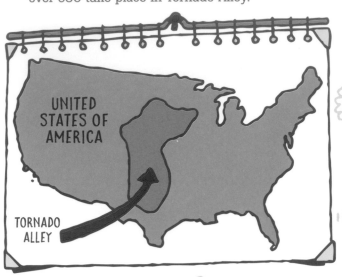

UNITED STATES OF AMERICA

TORNADO ALLEY

When is "tornado season"?

In Tornado Alley, most twisters strike from May to late June. The peak time of day for twisters is from 4 to 9 pm.

What should I do to protect myself during a tornado?

- Move calmly to a storm shelter or basement.
- If a shelter is not available, find a windowless interior room. Crouch down and protect your head.
- Keep away from windows.
- If traveling, get out of your vehicle and lie flat in a ditch or depression.

Can forecasters give advance warning that a tornado is on its way?
The US National Weather Service can give a twister alert
13 minutes ahead of time.

Are there different types of tornadoes?
Sure! A twister that happens over water is called a **waterspout**. A **dust devil** is
a tornado where hot air swirls up from the ground. It is full of dust and debris,
rather than water droplets.

What's a
tornado's
favorite game?

twister!

WATERSPOUT

DUST DEVIL

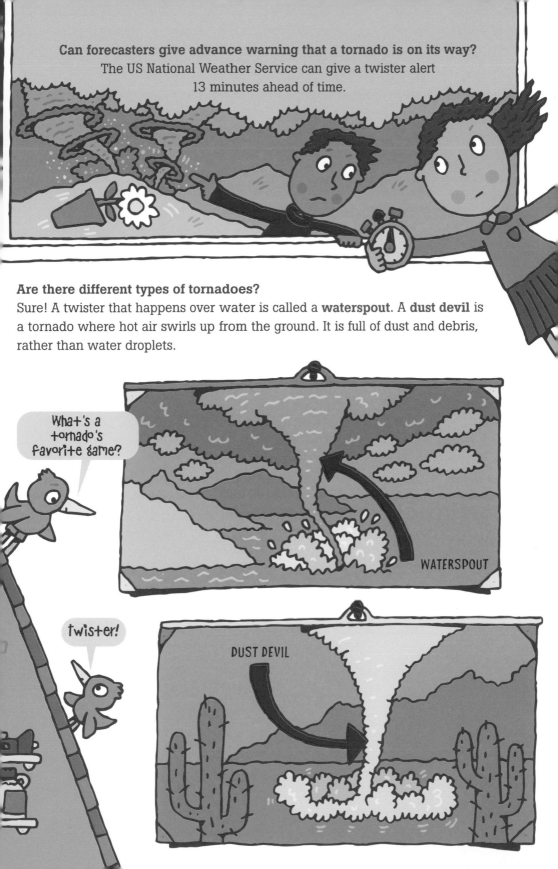

SPECTACULAR SANDSTORMS!

Time for a trip to the desert. Let's see what these vast sandy spaces have in store!

What's a sandstorm?
It's a strong wind that blows sand and dust from a bare, dry surface, such as a desert. These fine particles hang in the air and then can fall hundreds of miles away as a layer of silt.

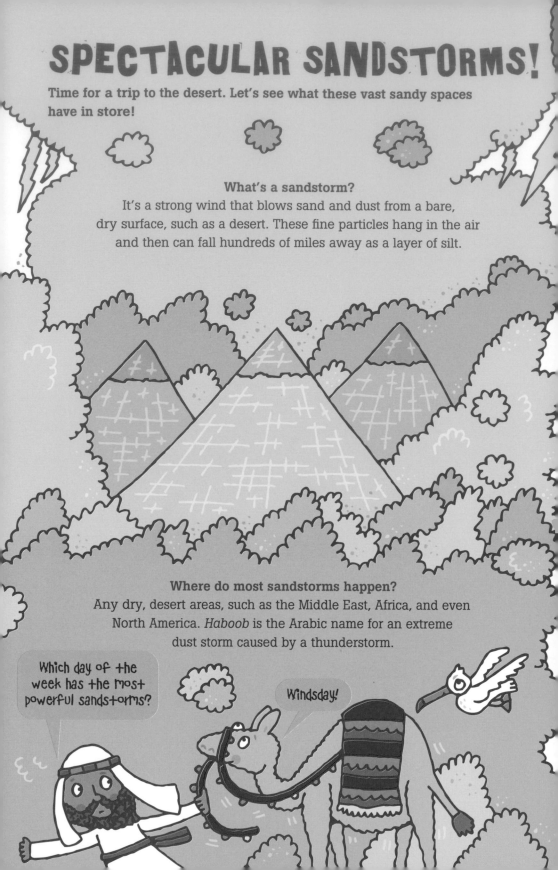

Where do most sandstorms happen?
Any dry, desert areas, such as the Middle East, Africa, and even North America. *Haboob* is the Arabic name for an extreme dust storm caused by a thunderstorm.

Which day of the week has the most powerful sandstorms?

Windsday!

Are sandstorms dangerous?

Yes! They often strike without warning, and dust from them can rise up thousands of feet (anywhere from 1 to 7 km) in the air. The dust can travel huge distances. In 2018, a sandstorm blew 1,607 miles (2,586 km) from the Sahara Desert to Sochi, Russia, where the snow was coated in an orange dust!

What are the worst sandstorms in history?

A 50,000-man Persian army was supposedly swallowed up by a catastrophic sandstorm in an ancient Egyptian desert. In the US, the **Dust Bowl** drought was one of the worst natural disasters in the 20th century. On April 14, 1935 (or **Black Sunday**, as it became known), the Great Plains endured the largest dust storm in American history. Terrifying winds of 60 mph (96.5 kph) whipped up an estimated 300,000 tons of soil. 250,000 people fled the region, and the damaged farmland took many years to recover.

HEAT WAVE

Let's find out what's hot and what's not!

We know that Death Valley, California, recorded Earth's highest temperature. But where is the hottest _inhabited_ place on our planet?
You'd have to move to Dallol, Ethiopia, in Africa. With an average temperature of 94°F (34.4°C), this alien-looking environment features bubbling ponds of yellow and green acidic water, hot springs, and two active volcanoes.

Which sizzling spot has experienced the world's longest heat wave?
Let's head to Marble Bar in Australia. Back in 1923, this town set the record with 160 consecutive days of 100°F (37.8°C) or above. Phew!

We know that snow, ice, and fog cause transport problems.
Is scorching weather dangerous to traffic, too?
Most certainly. Planes are grounded if temperatures hit 119°F (48°C), as extreme heat can harm a plane's equipment. Heat waves can cause roads to bulge and crack, and metal railroad tracks to expand, warp, and buckle, increasing the danger of trains derailing.

What are the dangers of a long heat wave, with minimal rainfall?
Drought. A lengthy period of unusually dry weather can be devastating. Crops can fail, causing famine and forcing people to leave their homes and countries in search of food. The worst drought famine in history saw 13 million people die in northern China between 1876 and 1879, when the rains failed for three years in a row.

What health problems can be caused by extremely hot weather?
A heat wave can affect anyone, but the elderly, young children, and people with medical conditions can become dehydrated, overheat, and suffer from heat exhaustion and heat stroke. It's best to stay shaded, drink lots of fluids, and take cool baths or showers.

What other impacts can a heat wave have?

Record temperatures can cause hot, dry conditions, leading to destructive wildfires. In recent years, California's wildfire season has seen almost 900,000 acres of land burn, destroyed 129 million trees, and caused the deaths of more than 100 people.

WHAT ARE THE BEST WAYS TO AVOID STARTING A WILDFIRE?

If you're camping, make sure an adult puts out the fire completely before you sleep or leave the site.

Take extra care of lanterns, stoves, and heaters.

Do not throw away matches on, or near, park grounds.

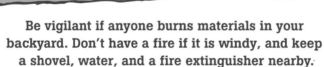

Be vigilant if anyone burns materials in your backyard. Don't have a fire if it is windy, and keep a shovel, water, and a fire extinguisher nearby.

If you see a wildfire, call emergency services, the local fire department, or the park service immediately.

What happens to animals in extremely hot weather?

It's important to look after our pets in a heat wave, as some animals are unable to cool themselves down in hot weather.

Use a pet-safe sunscreen on exposed areas, such as nose and ears.

NEVER leave animals in hot cars.

Put ice cubes in their water bowl.

Don't walk dogs at the hottest part of the day, and don't over-exercise them. Check the temperature of the sidewalk with the back of your hand.

Keep fish and reptile tanks out of direct sunlight, and change their water often.

Make a cool bed for your pet to lie on, with an ice pack or damp towels.

PLANET PREDICTIONS

It's time to take a look at the forecasts for the future. What might our weather look like in years to come?

Why might our weather change?
Temperatures on our planet are slowly rising due to global climate change, and a warmer world means that sea levels are rising.

Why is that important? Isn't warmer weather a good thing?
As Earth's ice and glaciers melt, islands and coastlines will begin to disappear underwater. When our oceans heat up, the water expands and takes up more space. Average sea levels have risen by 8 inches (203 mm) since 1880, and every year the sea levels swell by 0.13 inches (3.2 mm).

46

How does this affect the weather?

Higher sea levels mean an increase in extreme and unpredictable weather conditions, such as hurricanes, typhoons, and storm surges. Unstable weather is a serious challenge for farmers, who work hard to grow the food we all depend on. Millions of people in coastal areas are at risk from flooding, and rising seas are forcing people to leave their homes and migrate to higher ground.

What is causing this global climate change?

Homes, cars, and industry around the world burn huge amounts of oil and gas, called **fossil fuels**. During this process, **greenhouse gases** are released. These gases form a blanket around the Earth, trapping heat from the sun. This warms our planet and increases average temperatures.

CAUTION

FLOOD

What other factors play a part in global warming?

Rainforests are being cut down for wood and palm oil, and to build roads, mines, and dams. These trees are vital, as they absorb harmful greenhouse gases, then release oxygen back into the air. That's why these rainforests are called "the lungs of the Earth."

What is being done to reduce our dependence on fossil fuels?
We are harnessing the weather to supply alternatives to burning fossil fuels. For example, solar panels capture energy from the sun to produce clean and renewable power.

Are there any other ways that could work?
Wind can turn the blades of a turbine, which then spins a shaft that connects to a generator to make electricity. Some of the biggest wind turbines (windmills) are as tall as a 20-story building and can generate enough electricity in a year to power 600 homes!

How can I help combat the effects of global warming?
Check out these simple ways you can help the planet:

Use energy-saving lightbulbs and appliances.	Limit your car travel, if you can.	Reuse and recycle.	 Use less hot water. Take a short shower instead of a deep bath.
Try not to buy food or products with lots of packaging.	In the winter, put on a sweater and turn down the heating, and in the summer, use less air-conditioning.	Plant a tree. 	Turn off your electronic devices and read more books!

Now, you've come to the end. Time for some fresh air . . . whatever the weather!

How did you find the weather on your vacation?

I just went outside and there it was!

CHECK OUT ALL OF THE FANTASTIC FACTS IN THIS SENSATIONAL SERIES!